"I Was A Jerk!"

"I Was A Jerk!"

◆

True Confessions of a Divorced Husband

Blake Ramsey

iUniverse, Inc.
New York Lincoln Shanghai

"I Was A Jerk!"
True Confessions of a Divorced Husband

iUniverse books may be ordered through booksellers or by contacting:

iUniverse
2021 Pine Lake Road, Suite 100
Lincoln, NE 68512
www.iuniverse.com
1-800-Authors (1-800-288-4677)

Because of the dynamic nature of the Internet, any Web addresses or links contained in this book may have changed since publication and may no longer be valid.

The views expressed in this work are solely those of the author and do not necessarily reflect the views of the publisher, and the publisher hereby disclaims any responsibility for them.

(Pen name of author and title of book in its entirety are registered and copyrighted.)

(The phrase "Planet Marriage" has been officially copyrighted.)

ISBN: 978-0-595-46660-3 (pbk)
ISBN: 978-0-595-90955-1 (ebk)

Printed in the United States of America

Contents

A SPECIAL NOTE FROM THE AUTHOR

This book is written in an everyday common "I'm talking with you" style. I felt this was down to earth and would feel friendly to read. Please read as if I am talking to you, and with you, just as a friend would.

You'll notice a lot of three-dot groups … like that one. I'm trying to imitate everyday speech, and these three dots imitate the longer pauses we sometimes hear in everyday speech. They effectively **emphasize and separate** specific thoughts and ideas. To further meet this end, I used a lot of paragraph separation. This resulted in many very small paragraphs.

Some only one sentence.

The effort is to, again, emphasize a specific, individual thought for impact that will stick with the reader. **Bold** and *italic* fonts were used likewise to verbally emphasize, as in everyday speech, a word or idea that carries particular weight in that sentence.

The best public speakers are those that sound as if they are talking **with** the audience, and not **at** them. They also strive to present a collection of separate and specific ideas that stand powerfully alone, yet flow together harmoniously as one. This is the goal I have strived for. I hope you enjoy!

INTRODUCTION

I first wrote this book just for me. Then I realized that others, like you, might want it too.

Like me, have you ever acted like a jerk to your wife? And did you do it more than once? And if you haven't—would you like to read about someone who did?

Like the title says—that was me—I was a jerk. A husband ... jerk. I would now like to qualify though that this book is written for *everyone* ... jerks, non-jerks, married people, single people, divorced people, dating people, and everyone else alive and breathing. Why? It may be unlike anything you've ever read before.

I hope that this sometimes funny and many times thought-provoking confession will truly entertain you. But, I hope for more than that—I hope ... that it **leads** you.

To what? That's for you to find out. Go ahead—eavesdrop on my mistakes. Be my guest, and you'll find out all kinds of embarrassing things about me ... if that interests you. I could write about all of them, but the book wouldn't be able to fit in your trunk.

But whatever you do, don't enjoy this ... too much. It could be hazardous to your TV time.

Marriage … and *happiness* within that marriage … is truly a puzzle. A puzzle unlike any other! This book is my reflection, my contemplations … on how I failed this puzzle. It's about how I forgot to put the pieces where they were supposed to go. It's about how my finished picture … didn't make much of a picture at all. I ignored and/or disrespected too many of the necessary pieces, so my picture didn't come out right.

How else can a puzzle be completed, unless you have all the pieces for it? But what if you don't *have* all the pieces? This book … is about finding those pieces … and putting them together for yourself and your loved one.

The truth is—your marriage can become a gorgeous picture! It can become an *original*, a true work of art that you can call your own. I firmly believe that happily married people are the happiest people in the world.

"My Marriage Day"

I was married on a calm, crisp Saturday afternoon. It was quite a day for me … for it was my first real love, my first marriage. Surprisingly, like the weather that day, I was very calm. I knew so well and without any doubt that this was *the* woman, the only woman, for me.

Earlier that week, I had painstakingly created a huge living room length banner for our reception afterwards. I didn't know exactly what message to put on it, maybe something like "I hope you all brought expensive gifts!". But, I figured that might not go over very well. So, I ended up putting something short, sweet, and to the point. It simply read, "To Live, To Love, and To Learn … Together, Forever."

What I forgot to put after the word 'forever' in parentheses was "Or, until I discover that I'm really not ready to deal with marriage". That, unfortunately, would have been most appropriate.

Much pride has been swallowed with the writing of this book. To be bluntly honest, I feel like a complete failure, even though I know I am only a partial one. To my credit, I actually did a few good things while I was married. But I do know this … I could have done a *better* job as a husband. Truth be told … all divorced men could have been better husbands.

So, I feel this book is something that needs to be written. It needs to be told not just for me, but for the millions of divorced husbands who have or have not done the things that will be mentioned here. Perhaps they will find some understanding and some peace in their divorced state. And, I also feel it needs to be written for those on the <u>road</u> … to being divorced. It's also for those on the road to being married. If any of these descriptions fit you—read on. Perhaps you will all find a new thought—something different, something you'll remember. We're all in relationships, no matter who we are. Certainly all of us will find something about this book that is thought provoking. And let's not forget those who are *presently* married. This book is for them too.

"The World Of Marriage"

1492. When you hear this year, what's the very first thing that comes to mind? Our minds probably all think alike on this one. A New World was discovered by a man whose name is now very famous.

When you get married, you're discovering a new world just like he did. It is an adventurous and potentially beautiful world for all of its visitors. It can be truly magnificent, or, it can be downright dreadful. Or maybe … somewhere in between.

It's Planet Marriage. Yes, it is a world, even a planet, if you will. It, like our literal planet Earth, has its cycles, its turns, its ups, its downs, its fast times, its slower times, its hot times, its cold times. It has its seasons … its rain, its snow, its sun, its moon. Sometimes Planet Marriage is predictable, other times it is not. Just like weather here on Planet Earth.

Temperatures definitely vary on Planet Marriage, so much sometimes that you find yourself wearing a nice warm blanket and a coat for winter, but later in the *same* day, you'll be wearing a pair of trunks and sandals for summer. Have you ever experienced this in a relationship? It's a bit comical, but very true at times. The moods and 'weather' of your world—Planet Marriage—are that unpredictable sometimes. Our literal planet and its well-being depend on the behavior and respect of its dwellers, and so does planet Marriage. But in Marriage, there aren't 6.6 billion dwellers like here on Earth. Instead, (and thankfully), there are only *two*. But, sadly enough, it seems at times that these two on their planet Marriage can create more chaos and problems than everyone else on planet Earth! That is precisely why divorce is a household word nowadays.

Quite ironic, isn't it? Divorce being a 'household' word. So sad, and so true. The U.S. divorce rate is approaching 60% and beyond. Are you on your way to becoming a statistic as well? If not, I applaud your success.

Really though, marriages just don't last like they should anymore. They wear out way too quickly. There are just way too many problems in marriage without the proper **problem solving efforts** to match. This book ... can be used as a problem solver. It helps the reader to understand and address some of the most fundamental issues and problems that are found at the core of many relationships. I welcome you to turn the page.

I will now end the introduction with a warning. This book will challenge you in many ways. You can stop reading whenever you like.

I'd like to make it clear at this point that this entire book is non-fiction, and these are confessions and observations from a real person, namely me, who was *really* married to another *real* person.

All of the observations mentioned here are based on a real marriage that took place at an undisclosed place during an undisclosed time.

1

"I WAS VERY INSENSITIVE"

How was I not sensitive, you ask? How much time do you have today to read this? The answer to that could literally take all day. The chapter titles themselves are all ways in which I was very insensitive. The titles pretty much cover the forest of it, but as for the trees—here's a few:

> I wouldn't let her be herself. She was a beautiful girl, but I wanted her to think and act like a man and not be emotional. So when she was, I basically made her pay for it and not get away with it by being very nasty, distant, argumentative and cold. Instead of having empathy … I became her enemy.

> I was a totally, completely unrelenting nit-picker, constantly starting fights by overanalyzing things she said, reading more into them than what was there, and by generally looking for the negative in her instead of the positive.

> Probably the worst one—many times when she reached out to me for understanding, friendship and love … I simply wasn't available. That really sums it up. I was too busy being an insensitive husband.

And there's a whole lot more—but after a while it would seem redundant, especially since my insensitive ways are already thoroughly discussed throughout my book. In fact, this topic of sensitivity, and the lack of it, sets the tone and meaning for this entire book.

Sensitivity. Does anyone really have it? It's hard to get, but awesome to have. When I personally think of 'sensitive', I think of a person reading Braille. How much more sensitive can you get than that? The reader of Braille reads tiny, tiny bumps with his fingertips, deciphering minuscule differences in the almost microscopic spaces between the bumps. And he does this over and over again, practicing, practicing, practicing.

You might think at first that this constant grueling demand for sensitivity from his fingertips might backfire. If he did it long enough, would he become *less* sensitive from all the work and wear on his fingertips?

There's the first gem revealed in this book. Instead of becoming less sensitive from the effort, he becomes *more* sensitive. His **skill of sensitivity** *increases* … but only with use! This is a gem of wisdom of which I was truly clueless.

And so it is with people in relationships. It's true … being sensitive is a form of work, just as reading Braille is. But do our hands, our *hearts* … get calloused from being sensitive? Not at all. It may sound ironic, but our hands, our hearts, our minds … they all become *more* sensitive … from the ***work of sensitivity***.

I am very impressed by a Braille reader. His or her skill of sensitivity is most amazing. Is there anything *weak or unmanly* about it? On the contrary, there is nothing but ***strength*** about it. If you don't think it takes strength and amazing skill … go for it. Try it yourself. See how much strength, skill, and patience it takes … *to be sensitive*.

We men know these truths … but why in the world do we sometimes still equate sensitivity with unmanliness?

It is a highly complex discussion, because sensitivity is such a small word for such a big thing. Sensitivity, whether it is manifested in tender human emotion (it does happen with men now and then, or so I've heard), whether it is just the right gravity from Earth pulling on the Moon (so we won't crash), whether it's just the right amount of oxygen in our air (so you won't blow up when you light up)—sensitivity relates to *every* aspect of *every* day of *everyone's* and *everything's* life. Sensitivity, with its presence, or vacancy, affects everything animate and inanimate either for the good, or for the bad.

But for us animates, or people, I'll define sensitivity as 'The ability, and **_desire,_** to accurately recognize and *emotionally* respond … to the needs and desires of people *other* than ourselves."

I've sat and wondered about this for a long time, and I think the answer to why men are the way they are about sensitivity—could be summed up with this—many times we simply don't like to put up with anyone different than ourselves and our own masculine, non-feminine ways. When we think this way, we men then give ourselves a license … *to lack empathy*. As stated earlier, I was very guilty of this. And to add, I even felt justified in being guilty. That's another problem I had too—being guilty of emotional misdemeanors or worse … and then feeling justified in my wrong behavior.

No, I wasn't that way *all* the time, but much of the time I was. For instance … I hardly ever cried, so why should she cry … right? I rarely got emotional over what I thought were trivial matters, so how in the world could *she* possibly do such a thing? *I* was not subject to the same hygienic needs as she was, so why should her needs in this area have concerned me much? The kitchen was *her* room, so she was completely responsible for maintaining it, right? Etc., etc., etc.

Right? Wrong.

I suppose I was not only a jerk in these issues, but perhaps an even more accurate phrase would be appropriate—I was a stereotypical male chauvinist. What an ugly label, but I did fill it nicely.

To be sensitive to her needs, I believe that we are required to do four things—we must first *observe* ... and then we must **acknowledge and understand ...** what her needs are—from **her** point of view. Remember, as I did not—that her point of view, her mind ... is not ours. Her thoughts are different, her perspective is different. In my marriage I did not use this information—I ignored it. The fact is that most of the time when I should have been observing *my* wife's needs ... I was instead observing the TV or a phone call. If this is you, perhaps you should get off the phone, and give her the remote. She'll have a nice place she'll want to put it.

And too—if our *heart* isn't in it—in being sensitive—it simply won't be enough. Our act of sensitivity won't last, because it will be just that—an *act*. And I know that from doing it myself. But if it is real, if our heart is caring about and aware of her needs, we will then fulfill our fourth and final requirement to become skilled at sensitivity. We will *emotionally respond*. We will do something about it, unlike me. We will <u>act</u> on the emotional needs ... of the one we love. We will have the feelings that will motivate us to be sensitive. Really, do we love her, or what, guys? But, this brings a vital point to the fore. Many men say they love their wife dearly, but yet, if you were to ask their wives about their man's manifestations of sensitivity, you may hear otherwise. Why?

Men may indeed love their wives. But perhaps many simply *do not know how* to be sensitive. And they are better men than me—I knew how but still didn't. On the other hand, perhaps all men *do* really know how, but for various reasons, they simply do not know the **value** of this skill, and therefore are not concerned with using it. They may not realize how vastly important sensitivity is to their wife. But if a man were to think this way and not really be concerned about sensitivity with his wife, I would quickly ask him, "Do *you* appreciate it when she is insensitive to *you?*"

Of course not. We know how important sensitivity is to *us*, so logically, it must be important to our wives. A very, very wise man long ago once gave us a rule made of gold that speaks volumes on this universal principle of fairness. But, even if a man honestly doesn't know how to be sensitive, I provided its definition as a formula, a rule of thumb. But really though, sensitivity, or the lack of it, really just boils down to one thing.

Selfishness. It is the ultimate barrier to sensitivity. **Un**selfishness ... is the ultimate *invitation* to sensitivity. This is the last part of the definition which turns our key ... and opens our door.

We have to put others ... *before ourselves*. Especially ... our wives and loved ones. We have to be ... **un**selfish. Boy is it difficult at times. Why is it so hard? I'll tell you why—To be sensitive, thereby being unselfish and putting someone else's needs before our own ... means that the other person, for a moment, is *superior* to you. Yes, at times we really should elevate our loved one as superior to us, prioritizing their need ... over ours.

Equal, yet superior when needed. Yes, my wife was my equal partner, and she should have been viewed as *more important than me* ... at times. That's sensitivity in a nutshell, and it is also an excellent structural principle for marriage that I personally recommend for both sides—male and female—if they desire success.

If at least we **try** to be sensitive, that's a wonderful start, and I give you credit for it. It's not always easy, and sometimes it's just plain hard. The fact is I'm still trying to get better at it myself, and I'm sure I'll continue to try until the day I die. If we all just keep at it, like that Braille reader—you and I will only get better and better at the art of sensitivity, much to our own life's benefit and to the happiness of those we love.

2

"I WAS A BAD LISTENER"

I now realize that hearing and listening ... are not synonyms. They are not the same. To say they are the same would be like saying an apple *seed* ... is the same as an apple. They're similar, they're from the same idea, but one is much more mature than the other. The apple has done the work of growing from the idea, the seed ... but the seed by itself has done very little, if anything. The seed could be compared to just hearing ... and not listening. I guess I was a very bad seed.

Basically, when I was hearing her, *I really wasn't doing anything.* My body was doing it for me—because hearing by itself is really just an involuntary function, like a heartbeat. On the other hand, *listening* involves an active participation—a focused intent and willing attitude on the part of the listener. It involves a <u>voluntary</u> work on our mind's part. The listener is superior to the hearer because he is not interested in just the words ... but rather, he desires the meaning, emotion, and intellectual application of them.

Well, now that I've defined listening, why didn't I do it? Because it is not always easy, and honestly, I sometimes just didn't care, or I was just flat out too lazy to really listen and think about her words. Rather than listening, I sometimes just reacted, because *feeling is easier than thinking.* Once again—guilty as charged.

Oh yes—I 'heard' my wife all the time. But I didn't care enough … many times … to *really listen to* her words. I didn't look for the *true meaning* of her words, which promoted many misunderstandings between us. This resulted in her being resentful and bitter towards me, which resulted in me feeling the same towards her afterwards. Our verbal relationship, in general, was like the proverbial dog chasing its tail, and many times this vicious cycle was created by a general lack of listening on my part. *'Listening laziness'* … is what I think I could call it now that I think about it. That most definitely described me.

When I think of some of our fiercest arguments, I think of the cartoon fight. The dog and the cat whizzing around each other in a white flurry of dust, making odd and disturbing noises, and all you see are occasional arms and legs popping in and out of the fray. And needless to say … I, the dog, wasn't *listening* to the cat. That was our marriage many times, verbally speaking.

Does this 'cartoon fight' occur with you and your loved one? If so, you are not alone. And if so, you no doubt want it to get better, just as I did.

Poetically speaking, if our eyes can 'listen' as much as they can see, they will 'listen' to the unseen clouds at night as the rain falls … knowing that they are the true source of the rain. Our eyes will 'listen' to the hidden sun at sunset … knowing that it is really still there, even though it is out of sight. Our eyes will 'listen' … to the waves as they wash upon the shore, knowing that they come from a source somewhere else, somewhere very far away.

I discovered that the words of my wife could be like those hidden clouds, the obscured sun, and those secret waves. Her words had a different source and meaning than I sometimes knew! That's why—I needed to listen.

So tonight, men, like every night, let's all kick up our feet, eat snacks, read the paper, ignore everyone around us, and then quietly watch TV. Let's do this instead of communicating, and listening, with our wives and loved ones. Sound like a good idea? Hopefully, you've been listening, and you know the answer.

Right about this time, perhaps some of you men out there have simply had it and are thinking, "Hey ... what about the things that *women* do wrong? What about *them* not listening to me?" We all know we can improve in our listening, and these reflections and observations about listening apply to women just as well. But guess what—I'm not a woman, and as a man who isn't a woman, I didn't make the mistakes I made as a woman! I made them as a man. And as a man, I write to myself and other men. But if women insist on reading this, then I suppose I have no choice in the matter. And whatever they have to say about what I'm writing—you guessed it—I'll be listening.

3

"I HARDLY SAID I WAS SORRY"

I remember, as I'm sure you do, when I was just a kid. There I was, standing by the window I just broke with my foul ball, waiting on the infuriated home owner to squash me out of existence. They finally came out, they didn't quite do all of that, at least not physically, and then right when I finally think they're done, here comes … Mom.

And she's just getting started. First thing out of her mouth was my favorite thing … "*Now you say you're sorry, young man!*". I was only seven, and of course, I promptly obeyed, not really caring if I meant it or not. I may have felt sorry, a little anyway, but more than anything I was just mad at his window for being in the way of my baseball.

In my seven year old mind, I was misunderstood and mistreated. It was **his** fault, not mine, right? It was his *window's* fault, right?

So here I am today, much older than seven. I'm big, grown up, mature and sensible. (That's actually just a rumor.) It's been decades, literally, since I've been childish and didn't want to apologize about my broken windows. So what do I do now when I break the 'windows' of my *adult* life?

Windows?

Someone else's feelings, someone else's dignity. Maybe even someone's belief ... that I loved them. These are all 'windows' that I can and did break ... but not with foul balls.

These 'windows' were the heart and spirit ... of my wife. These were broken ... with foul *words*.

Sometimes I found myself throwing mean words at her—randomly through the air—just like vicious foul balls that carelessly broke whatever was in their path. Perhaps you also do it or have done it. Perhaps we all have done it. But that doesn't make it right. So what do we do about it when it *does* happen? How should I have made it better?

Well, it's hard to say.

Literally.

It was very hard for me. I didn't say "I'm sorry" ... enough. As a man, it can be really tough to say it! It's even harder to really mean it. To say it is to **admit** your mistake, to admit you were wrong. I didn't like it when I was seven, and I don't really like it now. I venture to say that many of us don't.

But we're adults now, right? We live in the real world, and we know what *being responsible for our actions* means. And especially ... when it comes to our wife and loved ones. I knew that being responsible meant being able to say I'm sorry when necessary. Or in other words, saying I'm sorry to someone, especially my wife—was more than an option—it was my responsibility.

And not just *feeling* sorry … but **acting** like it … to the offended person. And then, not only acting like it … but really *meaning* that action as well—these are what make an apology authentic. Isn't it crazy though? I had the audacity to blame her when many times it was plainly my fault! Just like I did when I was seven—we can blame other people's feelings, or 'windows', for simply being in the way of our careless words, our foul balls. As if it was really their fault, when they are actually *the victim*! I should have been asking myself, "How old **am** I, anyway?"

No matter if we're seven years old or seventy years old, or anywhere in between … we all know how it feels to be apologized to. We understand the gratitude we feel for the offender … after the sincere apology is made. This is the true power of the apology, when it is really meant. It can cool a fiery amount of anger inside of us down to a low simmer, or even less … in a relatively short time. In terms of payoff, I'd say it's a pretty good investment—the apology. Looking back, I see now how much I missed, and messed, because of not investing in the apology.

When I actually did apologize, everything usually got better. For both sides, the giver and the receiver—dignity was at least partially restored. She felt better about me, and in her mind, to some degree, she was reminded that she was *still worth the effort.* Upon reflection, I think that too was a vast shortcoming on my part—not making her feel really worth something. Worth my time, my interest, my energies … really, I didn't make her feel like she was worth **me**. She didn't feel like she *was worth my life*—no, instead, because of my behavior, she felt detached, separate, at arms-length from my life, a glorified acquaintance that I was physically attracted to. My lack of apologizing in conjunction with many other things led her to these feelings, and rightfully so.

It is a beautifully complex event—the apology—and I truly believe that it takes a real man to do it. But, the fact remains that I still didn't apologize for many things I should have. I hurt her feelings, I made her angry, I was late, and I didn't do what I said I was going to. Did I apologize? Now and then, maybe. Instead, I usually just copped out by telling her the cliché—"You shouldn't be so sensitive", or, "don't worry about it." I was sort of like that seven year old boy with the baseball … I blamed her for being in the way of my action. Stupid, but true. Even if my action was inappropriate, I still found ways to weasel out of apologizing and *being responsible for my actions*. I found ways to keep what I thought was pride … by not apologizing.

Like me, do you have, or have you had, a strong or possibly morbid fear of apologizing in your relationship? Perhaps you feel that your *pride* … is better to keep than apologizing to your loved ones. If so, I would ask you, reader, to no longer be afraid of these two words. Perhaps you are already not afraid, and that is wonderful. The Spanish seem to be brave in this regard. They have a most interesting way of saying this phrase, and it sheds insight into its true meaning for us who speak English. When the Spanish say "I'm sorry", they're literally saying "I regret it" in English.

It is *good* to regret things, especially when necessary. And if we do regret something we have done, we shouldn't wait forever to say it like I frequently did. The longer I waited to apologize, the less it seemed I meant it when I finally said it. I may have actually meant it, but to the ears of my wife, it was diluted and watered down. When it comes to apologies, I now know that sooner is usually better than later.

Take it from a person who is sorry … he wasn't sorry. Take it from a person who lived, for the most part, without regret of his inappropriate actions towards his wife. This life of a general lack of regret did not make me happy. On the contrary, it was shallow, and it was emotionally unhealthy for me.

I propose to you something new. I propose that … not saying you're sorry … is **not** a privilege! To avoid it may seem the easy way, the prideful way out at the time, but I assure you, you're only hurting yourself and the ones you owe the apology to. Rather, I hope that you one day know and learn how to regret, and know how to do so with your heart. This is not easy, and I am still getting better at it. But with time and practice, life has become much better for me in my current relationship because of being a healthy and willing apologizer. I hope the same goes for you as well.

I firmly believe, and many scientific studies show—that people who know how to regret, to take back, to correct, and to make things right with others—*are the most mature and interesting people in the world.* Their lives are fuller, more meaningful and more fulfilling. Like me, would you like to join them and have a better life because of it?

The *skill of regretting* is to be highly valued in these people. It is a skill, not of the academic mind, but of the emotional heart. It allows the bearer of it to be humble, to learn from their mistakes, and to think of the feelings of others besides themselves. This is the skill we all must acquire, and especially those of us with families. If we do not, we will pay the consequences. But if we do … we will reap the rewards!

I will conclude with some very sobering food for thought. If you or I can't say we're sorry, if you or I have to be right all the time, and if you or I can't ever admit our mistakes … how do we really expect to be loved? And even if we are loved while being this way, how do we know we wouldn't be loved *so much more* … if we just learned how to apologize?

4

"I TOOK HER FOR GRANTED"

To 'take someone for granted' means, basically, to fail to appreciate the person, what they do, their *value as a whole* ... simply from overfamiliarity. We become *so* familiar with our partners, we're with them so much and know so much about them in so many ways ... they can become *less special* to us in our minds. Isn't that sad? And if you look up the phrase in the dictionary, you may see my picture as the definition, because it's exactly what I did with my wife.

Taking her for granted involved more than just apathy from overfamiliarity. It also implied a severe lack of appreciation, and I can prove it.

The word 'granted' means 'given', such as in an educational grant where a student is *given* a certain amount of money to go to college. And as for the other part of the phrase—which do we do when a gift is given to us? *Receive* it, or, *take* it? Which sounds better?

We *receive* it. It is a gift. How could it be a gift ... if we were **taking** it? It would then no longer be a gift.

Thus, we come back to our phrase. I don't ever recall my wife telling her friend in disgust, "I'm so sick of my husband. He's always *receiving* me for granted." I know it almost sounds comical. Because when the word 'receiving' replaces the word 'taking', we now have an entirely new concept. This contrast now shows us what is really going on. When I *took* her for granted, I was presumptuously and selfishly *taking* the gift of her person … and not gratefully and appreciatively **receiving** it. By taking her instead of **receiving** her, she and what she did … was not recognized as the gift that it many times was!

Think about it for a minute. (Don't worry—I'll join you) Do we really think this is what she wants? I know for a fact it isn't, and I know it from experience. (My current wife will heartily agree) Whether it is a wonderful meal, a great job cleaning the house, a great job getting the kids ready for school, being nice and sweet to us (even when we don't deserve it), doing a great job at work, just being a good person in general, or any *other* good thing she may do for her husband … these are all gifts not to be taken for granted! And that's why I should have been asking myself all along—"Am I *taking* her … or **receiving** her?"

When guys take their women for granted like I did, that's when she feels small, like background … like woodwork. And I think it's a fair statement to say that woodwork … isn't happy. It wants to be more. And I have learned from my experience that **receiving her and what she does with gratitude**—that is, not taking her for granted—is what it takes to make her feel … like more.

5

"I WASN'T HER FRIEND"

First, let's talk about how we treat our *other* friends, the ones we're not married to.

Isn't it most interesting that we treat our friends so well, so many times, even in the face of difficulties? Even more interesting is the fact that we treat strangers, who could be seen as potential friends, with even *more* courtesy and respect, for the most part.

Aren't we humans strange? We hardly know a person, we just met them, and we are very, very courteous, as we are eager to make a good impression. We overlook almost every flaw, ironically, because we don't know them yet. We wouldn't dare get mad at them or treat them disrespectfully … because we barely know them.

Hmmm.

They become our friends, in time. We know them much better now, and we are far more familiar with them. We actually care about them now, and they are important to us. Their life has meaning to us. So what do we do? We now feel it is okay to talk back to them, have an attitude now and then, and maybe even get angry with them occasionally. Not all the time, probably just a little, but we definitely do it.

We like them well enough … to view them in a moderately negative light at times.

Let's say time went on, you really got to know this person even more, and you ended up liking them so much that you married them! Well congratulations, that's great!

But … are you *still friends*?

Unlike the brand new acquaintance mentioned earlier, I did not always treat her with dignity and respect. Unlike that same acquaintance who later became my friend, I did not make our bad times only now and then. I was now in love with her, and I was on the *highest* level of relationship. I should have now treated her as far superior … better than I *ever* would have treated that new acquaintance or friend.

Instead, I treated her … like she was **less** than them.

Even though I loved her, many times I didn't treat her *nearly* as well as I would a friend! Is this you? I see it all around me. Go to your local mall, or anywhere there's a lot of people. You might very well see married people and dating people treating each other like only married and dating people can—badly, harshly, disrespectfully and/or with contempt. They may display a very obvious lack of patience with the other, a very disagreeable attitude, and a general overall apathy towards their very existence—with all the facial and body expressions to back it. If you watch them, you will soon ironically know that they must be 'together' in a relationship, because if it were otherwise … they wouldn't be treating each other so badly. Does that make any sense?

It is most definitely food for thought. Why did I … why in the world do *we* … many times treat the ones we love … worse than someone we *don't* love? Perhaps I can offer a mental exercise for this dilemma: Forget you're in love, forget all the drama involved in love, just for a few hours, preferably the whole day. Pretend … that your wife is just a new acquaintance, and see if you treat her any differently. I know it sounds strange, maybe impossible, but try it. Be an actor—see how the show comes out. (My current wife loves it when I do this)

Upon doing so, would you now be opening the door for her at a store? Would you now be saying "Excuse me", or, "Please", when appropriate? Would you now be apologizing more often? Would you now have more friendly, cordial, and accommodating tones in your voice in everyday conversation (like you would with a stranger)? Would you now be in such a hurry to judge her, thinking the worst? Rather, wouldn't you now give her the benefit of the doubt if at all possible (like you would someone you *didn't love*)?

Would you now be eager and anxious to make a good **impression**? (Like you would a stranger, again, that you **didn't** love?)

The fact is—irony of ironies—most of us would treat our significant others better … **if we didn't love them**. That is completely ridiculous, illogical, and just plain wrong. But I still did it.

Logic should have told me to be far, far more interested in impressing my wife than I would a mere stranger. I lived with her, she was my closest associate, literally, and she was supposed to be my helper, my partner, my friend—for life. Not only should I have loved her more than anyone else, but in addition—she also loved **me** … more than anyone else! She gave me reasons, she gave me *evidence*, to love her back! I had no reason, I had no evidence ... to treat a stranger better than I would my wife.

Common courtesy is defined as words and actions that respect the dignity, equality, and importance of our fellow human beings. Common courtesy should not have been forgotten or infrequently called upon when I was married and in love, on the contrary—it should have been **all the more** remembered. I would urge all married people to ponder this point.

My solution was right in front of me, but I ignored it. Now that I'm older and see it—I feel the solution is timeless, and it applies to everyone who is married, and best of all—it is ingeniously simple. We all learned it growing up. It is this—when we were children, friends acted certain ways to other friends. Friends were recognized ... *by the way they treated each other*. That was the wisdom that made sense in the mind of a child! If people didn't act like friends ... then well, they usually weren't!

It is all too plain to see that even now, as the adult that I am ... I can still learn from children.

6

"I WAS NEVER THERE"

"Honey, where 'you going tonight, and when will you be back?"

Silence.

More silence.

"I'm just going out ... I'll be back whenever ..."

Sound familiar? The physically and many times emotionally unavailable husband? That was me.

I was gone so much—it was a crime. As stated elsewhere in this book, in my mind I was still single. A single man comes and goes as he pleases without having to answer to anyone. But then, when he gets married, that, well, changes just a bit. And it should—because his life no longer just belongs to himself, for now he permanently shares it with another. That's called marriage.

Looking back, I realize how often I used the front door literally as an escape route ... to get away from us. Really, in effect—to get away from me, because I was the source of our problem more times than not. Sure, I wasn't always to blame, but whoever was at fault had nothing to do with my responsibilities as a husband. I was still the husband, and husbands handle things when it comes to husbands and wives. That is, if they're really trying to be a husband. As for the other kinds of husbands, the category that I was fitting in—they take the easy way—the *run away*. Sure, like all couples, we had arguments, disagreements, differences of opinion, different agendas, different plans, different needs, etc. But when these differences came to light and when they resulted in some emotional conflict—which is normal in marriage—I basically wanted very little or no part of it. I didn't want to do the work that sometimes—*many* times—marriage requires. So … I just left. And soon, because I used the door so much … our relationship began to turn into something about as thin as that door, about as small as that door.

I realize now that I created **more** pain and problems … by trying to *run away* from problems. And really, looking back, the problems that I *thought* were problems … weren't always that big of a deal! In my immature mind and state, I made them bigger than they really were, thereby making them worse … than they really were … thereby making **us** worse … than we should have become. If I would have stuck around and took the bad equally with the good, then like my current marriage, I would have little to do with the front door. Why? Because I wouldn't need it. I would have been just fine and happy inside—*not outside*—my house of marriage. I now know that a marriage can become happy, huge, substantial, formidable … as big as a house! And I also understand that it can become as small … *as the front door.*

To all those married readers, I wish you the best in your efforts to spend quality time with each other on a regular basis. I hope all of you are best friends, unlike me who felt that I was one of two people who simply 'had' to live together. If you have made or are making the same mistakes I've made, there's no time like the present … to change. If in your heart you know you need to be there more for her, then be smarter than me and do it … before it's too late. Because I remember the day when it was too late for us. And I remember knowing … it was my fault.

That was not a good day.

7

"I HARDLY EVER SAID I LOVE YOU"

I definitely failed in this as well. But I bet I know what men are thinking out there—"She already knows it! I tell her once in a while, and that's all she needs. Why do I need to repeat myself?".

Men, what if your wife says she loves *you*? (More than once a year ...) How do *you* feel?

Sure ... you already knew it. After all, you're married! That's enough—that says it all. So really, her words are a complete waste of time. They would have zero impact on you, your mood, and your relationship.

That would be ... wrong. Even though I myself did like to hear it and it did affect me for good—I in proper double-standard fashion ... *didn't say it back to her.* To illustrate the contradiction and hypocrisy of this ... what if your wife goes out and buys you that brand new pair of dress shoes for work you've been desperately needing? When you open the box, do we respond with, "Well gee honey, I already knew these shoes were on the rack at the store. And you knew I would enjoy them. So why did you have to go out and buy them and remind me how much I wanted them?".

Therefore, we get the statement, "Why did you have to go and say 'I love you' when I already knew it?" Could we get any more absurd here? I doubt it. Should I have thought of this earlier? Yes.

The point is … receiving those shoes as the gift that they are … is a good thing! And believe me, the words "I love you" are a better thing, a very *unique* gift. A gift—in a class all of its own. A gift … beyond material. Married women want this gift, but even more importantly—they *need* it. My wife not only wanted it and needed it—she also deserved it!

That should have been enough reason for me to say it freely … but it wasn't. I had another problem. To have said it, I would have had to swallow my pride. But in swallowing it, I now know that I would have gained something better—a *different* kind of pride. It is a very healthy pride to have … and it would have allowed me, in fact, encouraged me … to say these three words to my wife. It's the pride … in **knowing that we're not too proud** … to say it. Proud of not being proud. Interesting, awkward perhaps, but it is very true, very real, and very fulfilling. I now know this … years after the fact.

The saddest thing of all is when a man really truly does love his wife … but simply just can't, or won't, say it. That was me for the most part. The wife of such a man is probably hurting, aching, because of not hearing these words from the man she loves. She may secretly be wondering things like, "Well, I know he does … but why doesn't he say it? Am I doing something wrong? Does he secretly regret marrying me? Does he … wish I was someone else?" And on and on and on her thoughts can go. Maybe she's thinking these things, maybe she's not. Whether she was or not, I still should have said it!

And if you truly do love your wife, which deep down, I hope you do …
I'd recommend saying it tonight.

8

"I WAS A VERY POOR COMMUNICATOR"

When we were first married, we called each other every day. I distinctly remember one of my clients almost laughing at the frequency of our calls. They couldn't believe we called each other at least twice every day, and usually three times.

If nothing else, I would just call her to tell her I was thinking of her. I was doing that nice stuff husbands are supposed to do. And what's more, I wanted to. I really meant it, and it made me feel good to let her know how I felt. I was guilty of good things like that on occasion, believe it or not.

But, as time went on, everything began to change. After several months, I began to not call her everyday like I used to. The first signs of problems in our marriage were becoming evident, and I was beginning to back away from her as I slowly realized I didn't want to be around her nearly as much as I did before. The fact is—I was secretly wanting to be single again.

But that certainly does not excuse me from being rude. I ignored her pages she sent me constantly when I was out late, and of course, later than I said I'd be. I ignored her pages a hundred times if I did it once. I began, very sadly, to not value her attention and care. Isn't that awful? I think so. Upon reflection, I know for a fact that she certainly did care about me, and communication was one way she showed it! How obvious that should have been, but I was becoming too selfish to really see it.

In fact, I began to resent it. I began to be irritated at her need for me! Can you believe it? When she was paging me, wanting to know where I was and when I'd be home, she was showing love. She was showing she needed me. Did I appreciate it? Hardly. As the saying goes ... I blew her off. And I would ask husbands—**don't do what I did**.

Even if you really aren't the talkative type, or you're simply not in the mood to talk, don't dismiss or forget why she's really calling you or wanting to talk to you. She's probably doing it—because she loves you. Maybe it's true that she wants to talk more than you personally do, but guess what—*she's not you*. Talking to her, perhaps more than you see as necessary ... could very well be a part of the marriage that you agreed to. It's a part of life.... *married* life ... that you chose and are living. My advice is to accept it and enjoy it. And if you can't, then learn to. Because believe me, if you ever get divorced down the road, you'll probably miss it. There could very well come a time ... when you would simply *love* to hear the voice of someone who cares about you.

So, like me, don't wait until you're divorced to appreciate it. Appreciate it now, while you can. I have learned and believe, from experience, that willful, purposeful, and honest communication is the very *oxygen* ... that keeps married people alive. Just as a person needs to keep breathing to stay alive, married people need to <u>*keep communicating*</u> ... to stay married. I wish all of you the best in this regard.

9

"I WAS A CHRONIC CRITICIZER"

Would anybody in their right mind want to be a verbal 'wrecking ball' against their wife? She's a building, it's true. But she's not made of bricks.

Not stone bricks, anyway. The bricks of all people, including wives, are made of *emotion*. Wives … are *emotional buildings*. Wives are eagerly sensitive to their surroundings, and they would much prefer **mortar … to madness.**

Mortar? This is what *literal* bricks need. Mortar would be **con**structive criticism that is given to her in the spirit of building, of helping. Madness? The madness of the wrecking ball is what rips and tears bricks apart. This would be **de**structive criticism, criticism given <u>at</u> her in the spirit of tearing down, demeaning, and becoming less. This was my general method of choice—and it was highly destructive to our marriage. In small things and large, I found ways to verbally confront her about doing things the wrong way, doing them more **my** way—overall, I generally implied that what she said or did was almost always lacking in something. And of course—in my mind—**I** already had the thing that she was lacking. I had all the answers.

Yeah, sure—that's why I'm divorced now.

I should have realized then … that my wife was an <u>emotional building</u>. It was her makeup as a woman and as a human being! But I didn't acknowledge or respect that. Yes, she definitely did not like harsh collisions with 'wrecking balls', or negative, mean words from her husband. But I wouldn't have liked it from her either, so how could she have liked it from me? Simple logic should have been my teacher.

Yet, I still did it. Especially after analyzing all this and writing it on paper … I realize how insensitive, immature, and selfish I was as a husband.

My tones of voice were how I often smashed her as a wrecking ball would. They were mean and unkind many times. You know how a dog is, right? Not to be comparing any person to a dog, but you can say to the dog, "You are the ugliest creature on planet Earth" in a very nice, sweet, friendly tone, and your pet will be licking and jumping on you with affection. But, compare the opposite approach. You can say the words, "You are the most beautiful creature on planet Earth" in a very harsh, mean, and angry tone, and guess what? He won't want to play with you. He'll go somewhere else for that. Your original message, no matter how nice—is poisoned if the tone is harsh. And if animals are sensitive to tones, then humans … are all the more so. And when that human is your wife, well, how else does it need to be said? Looking back, honestly—when it came to communication, I think I was nicer to her pet than I was to her. That's embarrassing.

My wife needed to be <u>constructed</u>, not destroyed! And really, so did I! We all do, because we're all still growing and improving. We are all buildings in progress, and there are always more 'bricks' to be added to our humanity. But *too* many bricks? Too many bricks—too much criti-

cism—**and the original intent is distorted.** To its receiver, my wife …
the intention was lost.

Too many bricks, too much weight on her 'wall', or self, and then
something most important is lost. Balance is lost. Hers and yours. I was
being unbalanced in my giving of constructive criticism—it was just too
much—and she as the receiver, began to tumble and crumble downward
under the weight of my excessive criticism, exactly the same as a literal wall
of bricks would! My intention didn't matter. Now … **I** was the problem.

Without balance, I now know that constructive criticism … becomes
<u>destructive</u> criticism. Of course, it goes without saying that sometimes
even kind, sincere criticism can be received in anger. But usually, I have
found, that is because my timing was off. I gave the criticism at a time
when my wife was not ready to hear it. And, to be honest, I usually already
knew that ahead of time, but I gave it anyway. That too was one of my bad
male traits—to indulge in my logical self so much that I disregarded my
wife's current state of mind, and went ahead and dumped out whatever
criticism I logically felt was needed. That not only does not work, it also
completely undermines whatever benefit we hope our criticism would
yield. In this case, as in many others, with a woman you love … *sometimes
timing is everything.* That's just the way it is. Knowing this now—I should
not have tried to reinvent the wheel. Regarding this issue, I would advise
men to go with what you know, do what you know works—and chances
are, everyone will benefit.

And really, why is it that we usually criticize someone? Aren't we really,
actually holding it against them … for not being perfect? I was. I really
think most of us are guilty of that, even though we *know* that we ourselves
are far from perfect, and we know we ourselves have made countless mistakes. But somehow … we don't want anyone else to make any.

So, to conclude ... here's to all the buildings. Your buildings, my buildings, everyone's buildings ... *people, friends and families.* Let's together agree to see all people, especially our wives and loved ones ... as beautiful buildings in progress. If we really think that way and <u>*really believe it*</u> ... then unlike me, you will treat them accordingly, and better ... when it comes to criticism.

10

"I WAS TOO CONTROLLING"

Control is a part of life. It is a part of what makes us human—even down to each and every cell inside our bodies ... these all exist and thrive under controlled circumstances. The Earth itself, our home—it survives because of the delicate yet precise controls of the laws of science and nature. And indeed, even the most printed book in the world—the Bible—recommends us to exercise "self-control", claiming that in doing so you and I are in fact imitating God himself.

These are sobering thoughts. It would seem that control is a good thing, a '**should**' thing, would it not? It would seem that it is something necessary for life. It in fact is ... but what we also find in nature and science is that ... *control has limits*. It too ... needs control.

<u>**Control ... needs control.**</u> Or—control needs to be <u>managed</u> ... to bring about reasonable and balanced results. This is true in science and nature, so why wouldn't it be true for people? In nature, whether it is the study of the Earth's rotation and orbit in relation to the Sun and Moon, whether it is the behavioral study of atomic particles, whether it is the study of an elephant giving birth to its newborn, or even in the study of the rise and fall of the ocean tides—the words *control and freedom* ... can indeed be in the same sentence. Something being controlled, or managed and guided, and that same something having a considerable amount of

freedom to act ***within those managed guidelines*** ... is not only necessary, it is expected. And so it is too ... with humans. No matter if it is a husband/wife relationship, a parent/child relationship—even a human/animal relationship, this principle holds true.

I realize this now, and am continuing to realize it (with much credit and thanks to my wife) more fully as I get older in my current marriage. I won't lie—the tendency to overdo control is still there, but it is much more balanced, and reasonable, now that I myself have become well, a bit more balanced and reasonable. (I think) But yes, we have had more than one argument (a.k.a. information exchange) over this issue, and it is one of my many works in progress.

The truth is—many of us, like me, have a hard enough time of controlling and managing ourselves, but then in addition to this difficulty, we sometimes take on the task of trying to control someone else! And many times we do this ... whether they need it or not. Wow.

That was how it was in my marriage. But what's interesting is this—how I justified it. That's what I did with most of my mistakes in my marriage—I did them, and then I justified them! In the movies, there's nothing worse than a villain ... who thinks he's right. In my marriage, I was that villain. So the question arises—why did I have such an innate need of controlling her lifestyle and actions, and why is this control issue found in more than just a handful of men?

It hit me just the other day as I was driving my car. Here I was, going 65 miles an hour or so down the highway. I was going where I wanted to go, and I was doing it when I wanted to. That's what most of us would call freedom—the choice to do what we want, when we want, reasonably speaking of course. But as I was freely doing what I wanted ... I realized too that within this freedom was boundaries. In a sense, to attain this freedom, I had to be trapped. I had voluntarily limited myself inside the boundaries of the car ... to attain the freedom to go where I wanted. Really, I had to—there was no other way. And that's when it hit me. To be free ... I had to be controlled. And the only way I would choose to be controlled or limited ... was to be free to do what I want.

Linguistically and logically, this was a paradox. It took me my first two years of marriage to realize that I was creating this paradox—I was the creator of this emotionally unfair game. Basically, by my behavior, I was telling my wife, "Sure, honey, go ahead and get in the car to go where you want ... but don't move while you're in the car. Don't turn on the radio, don't turn on the air, not even the windshield wipers ... in fact—**don't even steer.** Drive the car, but don't steer. You're free to go ... even though you're not." This was a blatant contradiction, but nevertheless, it was my attitude.

Not giving her the right to do anything in the car could be compared to not giving her the right to do very much, if anything, in our marriage. We were together in our vehicle, our car, our marriage ... moving forward in our lives together. At times, we actually were going pretty fast, and the view wasn't always bad. But inside the car, on a daily basis, I was telling her not to do anything. Don't read, don't listen to music, don't turn on the air, don't talk (very much), don't watch portable movies ... don't do much of anything unless I approve it and okay it. Sure, we're together in this marriage, this car ... but that's where it ends. You're my wife, but inside this marriage, this car ... I pretty much make the rules and all the decisions.

I failed to realize that within our commitment, our marriage, our car ... there needed to be a considerable amount of freedom for her—otherwise, it would defeat its purpose. If you can't do anything inside the car, not even steer—then it's pointless … and soon you will stop and get out. Sure—you're moving, but it's no fun. In fact, it's miserable. Its own purpose of freedom and joy becomes defeated. Kind of like a stomach eating itself because it's hungry.

And worse than that was the hypocrisy I daily committed—the double standard of me … being able to have all the freedom **I** wanted in our marriage, our car—but *not her*. Like when I would go out at night whenever I wanted and as late as I wanted … by myself—but would never let her do the same. In fact, I preferred her to mostly, if not always, be home'waiting' for me whenever it was that I returned. And you guessed it—when I was gone, I rarely if ever called her to check in. And in fact when she repeatedly paged me, I almost always ignored it. But if she had treated **me** that way … oh, that would have been another story. That just wouldn't have worked at all. After all, I was the one with the cell phone—but I wouldn't let her have one. That was too much, too expensive. In fact, I had a beeper and a cell phone, and I hypocritically enjoyed her having to chase me and find me all the time, and conversely me not having to ever wonder where she was and find her on her cell. Because … she was either at work or at home. Just the way I liked it. The only other place she might have been was at her mother's—and even then I only liked that in small quantities.

With most elements in our marriage, small and large, I behaved very unfairly because of control issues. We would get into daily arguments even on petty issues, like what brand of lunchmeat to buy. And I usually started it. And a whole lot of it had to do with money. Counselors say that money and communication are the two biggest problems with couples, and ours was no exception. Our communication was handicapped to say the least, and again, mostly it was because I wanted her to be more like me, and think like a man. And—surprise—that just didn't work at all. And as far as money went, I almost daily put the squeeze on spending, which can be a good thing. But, as in many other things, I really overdid it, and in fact am still working on that tendency in my current marriage. Her freedom with money was nearly nonexistent. Sure, she had a house and a car and clothes and food, but I controlled all of it. Sadly, I remember her usually almost always having next to nothing in her wallet. And even more sadly, that's kind of the way I liked it. Control.

Well, now that you hate me, perhaps you're ready for the next chapter? Bur for what it's worth, I truly am more mature, reasonable and balanced in my current marriage regarding control. The fact that in my current marriage I've doubled the years of my first marriage may say something to my favor. But, I do slip now and then and relapse into my old tyrannical ways, and I still have to work on it. But now, in general, because of having less control issues, life is now better and more fun. For both of us.

11

"I JUST WASN'T ON THE TEAM"

A team ... is made of more than one. In marriage, it is made of two. That really pretty much sums it up. One person + one person ... does not equal one person. It might not take a brilliant mind to figure that one out—but it may just take a brilliant heart. And my heart wasn't brilliant, or present enough, in my committed relationship. And if that's the case, no matter who you are, like mine—your marriage <u>will</u> <u>not</u> <u>last</u>.

Why did I secretly think inside, although I was married, I was still single? Why does anyone do it? Think about it.

And then, after the dust and maybe three years clears and you're divorced or on your way to divorce—we then have the audacity to say, "Hey, what happened?" I know what happened—a sad thing happened. I was married to a woman I loved, but sometime after, I realized I loved someone else even more. Me.

Teams cannot work, do not work—in a selfish environment. So really, for her sake and out of respect for her as a human being, and to spare her from emotionally investing in me ... I just should have stayed single. I wasn't ready to be a team. This and many other things made me—you guessed it—act like a total jerk.

So if you're married, act like it. Be on the team. Or one day, like me, you'll be kicked off.

FOUNDATION

How does a literal, real home start? It starts with the <u>foundation</u> and all of its necessary preparation. When we had our home built, we saw them make the foundation and learned a few things in the process. It is complicated … it takes time. I learned that a foundation is much more than just a concrete block. It requires a certain kind of gravel, and special fluid with that gravel to make the concrete stay together.

If a bunch of concrete was just poured out in a square pattern and allowed to harden, it would indeed make a big square concrete block. But would it consistently and correctly hold a house upright? It would, but only for a short while. It would begin to crack soon. Sooner or later, **everything wouldn't be enough**.

That's exactly what happened with me and our marriage. Soon enough, everything wasn't enough. I really believe this is so because our foundation wasn't properly put together. I didn't know her long enough, we didn't date long enough. I got in a hurry, as many young people do with marriage. We didn't add the necessary 'gravel' to our concrete to make our foundation stable. Sure, I loved her and cared for her greatly, even though I inconsistently acted like it—but that love and care was not based on a true and accurate knowledge of who she *really* was. It was based on who I wanted her to be … who I *needed her* to be. Kind of like a fantasy, I suppose.

What could we compare the foundation to? What would the concrete be? It would be the outright love and need and yes, infatuation—for the other person. Yes, it is good, and it is very necessary. The attraction, need, and desire—and the spark from it all—certainly helps, and they are good things. But if that is all there is, it will not be enough. It needs to be coupled and complimented with extensive *knowledge, understanding, acceptance and insight* of the other person for who they really are. This is where I failed miserably. This … is where the other parts of the foundation come into the picture.

The gravel in your foundation could be compared to knowing and accepting all the 'small' and 'large' qualities of the other person, even the ones you think won't matter. (You know—the stuff that's just lying around) But they do. Gravel comes in all sizes, small, large, irregular, and everything in between. So do qualities, attitudes, mannerisms, inconsistencies, and peculiarities. It seems like an odd bunch of words, just like bits of oddly shaped gravel. But let me tell you, acceptance and realization of these hold the house up nicely, or irritation and rejection of these can sink the house nicely. The choice is yours. It was mine too—and I blew it.

Because … it's every single day. Every, every, EVERY day these irritations and irregularities exist with a couple and need to be dealt with in a good and constructive way. I know now that I chose to ignore, therefore not use, the 'gravel' in our foundation. I chose to ignore that I would have to deal with her irregularities and inconsistencies. I just didn't expect that going in to the marriage. I was just so satisfied with the concrete block … the need I had for her, the love I had for her … I thought that's all I needed. After all, love is all you need, right? It sounds good, especially in a song, but we all know it simply is not reality.

The gravel though … now *that's* reality. That's every day—that's human relations—irregular, inconsistent, and imperfect, very much different than the nicely square and perfectly shaped concrete foundation. And they *have* to be there, they have to exist … to hold the house up. For the house … to be real. Because if you ignore the 'gravel' going into the marriage, your 'house' won't stand up under the pressure. Everything … will soon not be enough.

The hardcore fact is—to live with someone you're in love with requires more than just love! Just as a car requires more to work than just gasoline, so do relationships require more than just love. Love makes a great fuel, but what about all the other parts in the engine?

Think about it. For both of us.

"IN MEMORY—A VERY SPECIAL WOMAN WHO DESERVED BETTER ... "

Why did I fall in love with her? My, my ... the feelings I had for her in the beginning. She was so very, very special to me. I didn't want her to leave my sight, literally. It felt, as the cliché goes, that I had found the other half of me, like I had been walking around all my life like an oddly shaped piece of puzzle, only half of a small picture. And then, somehow, she fit with me, and we made a bigger picture, together. That is definitely what it felt like, but feelings aren't necessarily based on reality, as we all know. But boy oh boy, it was a wonderful feeling. I mean after all, this was my first marriage.

She had many, many good qualities. She was very generous of her time and material things with others. She loved to give gifts to me and everyone she cared for.

I remember ... our first anniversary. We had hidden our gifts throughout the apartment before the big day, and the anticipation was a lot of fun. It turns out she had bought me over a dozen gifts! It was so much fun, and it made her happy to give. She was very kind that way.

She was very, very intelligent, having the ability to discuss almost any subject at any time. When we both were in the right frame of mind, we had some awesome conversations. Along with that intelligence came a great playfulness which I loved. She was very much like a playful little girl many times, which in large part is why I fell in love with her. She loved to laugh and joke and play … I remember this particularly in our first year of marriage. We would have the best wrestling matches on the bed … wrestling, pillow fighting and laughter for a long time.

Those were good times. She was my friend then, my pal. She wanted to do things with me, she admired me … she was interested in the one she loved. She truly wanted to be my companion.

She enjoyed taking walks in the park nearby our apartment. She wanted to share time with me that way quite frequently. Although I will admit that many of these walks ended up in a big argument, I remember the fact that she wanted to spend time with me. The intentions were good, even if the outcome wasn't.

She could really cook! And I didn't even have to ask. She enjoyed giving me the dishes I loved, and she made them exactly the way I liked. She enjoyed spoiling me that way. And if I wanted something she wasn't familiar with, she would gladly learn how to make it. She really did love to please that way.

She was very, very reliable and trustworthy. I could count on her word every time. If she said she'd be home at a certain time, I could count on it. If she said she would call, she would. She communicated very well, and it made things work the way they should in a marriage. I believe her true love for me, along with a caring respect, motivated her to be this way. In short, she did her part. And many times—more than her part.

And all she really wanted in return … was to be held and comforted, and for me to remind her that she was loved. And of course, for me to be a good husband. Which on a scale of 1 to 10 ... I would honestly give myself about a 5. In school, that was an F.

So like the title says—I was a jerk! What was I thinking? I wasn't. But, I am now—with my wonderful wife of six years. Things have changed for me—but only because I finally grew up ... and made better choices. And I sincerely hope, after reading this—that you are now thinking about *your* relationship ... and the choices _you_ ... are making. Thank you for reading.

978-0-595-46660-3
0-595-46660-5